9/87

A
NATURAL
MAN

A NATURAL MAN

The True Story of John Henry

by Steve Sanfield

With Drawings by Peter J. Thornton

DAVID R. GODINE   PUBLISHER   BOSTON

First published in 1986 by
David R. Godine, Publisher, Inc.
Horticultural Hall
300 Massachusetts Avenue
Boston, Massachusetts 02115

Library of Congress Cataloging in Publication Data
Sanfield, Steve.
A natural man.

Summary: Retells the life of the legendary
steel driver of early railroad days who challenged
the steam hammer to a steel-driving contest.
1. John Henry (Legendary character)—Juvenile
literature. [1. John Henry (Legendary character)
2. Folklore—United States] I. Thornton,
Peter J., 1956–   ill.   II. Title.
PZ8.1.S242NAT   1986   398.2'2'0973   85-45965
ISBN 0-87923-630-2

First edition

Printed in the United States of America

For my mother and father
and
for all those who told it, sang it,
wrote it, remembered it, and kept it alive

The day before he was born a rainbow stretched across the sky from east to west.

The night was black—as black as a crow's wing dipped in ink.

There was a red, copper moon that didn't give off any light, and the stars were a million years away.

Roosters crowed, dogs howled, and somewhere in the woods a wild creature screamed.

A huge, dark cloud came and covered the moon and stars.

Forked lightning and rain poured out of that cloud, and the thunder made a hammer out of itself that pounded the earth until the roots of the trees shook.

The Mississippi River ran upstream for a thousand miles, and John Henry was born.

Some folks say he was born with a hammer in his hand. Others say that's the first thing he reached for—a hammer hanging on the cabin wall. But everyone agrees he weighed thirty-three pounds when he first came into this world.

His daddy took one look at him and said, "That boy's gonna be a natural man. I can see that as plain as a row of cotton runnin' uphill. Yes sir, he's gonna be a natural man."

Starting so big, John Henry naturally grew fast and he grew big—so fast and so big that he was only two when he sat on his mother's knee for the last time. And that time John looked up and said, "Big Bend Tunnel on the C. and O. 'Road gonna be the death of me."

Of course, what John Henry said didn't make a whole lot of sense to his mother, but the way he said it set her to shivering like a cold, wet wind would do.

Even though it was still slavery time, John Henry's folks dreamed of something better for him, so they got him a teacher to give him music lessons.

They started with the banjo, but as soon as John Henry grabbed it he snapped the neck like a piece of dry kindling wood. They tried the piano next, but when John began to play his fingers smashed that poor piano to bits. He was already that strong. Finally they tried singing, but as soon as John Henry raised his voice he raised the roof with it. That was the end of his music lessons, and that was the last time John Henry ever sang indoors.

By the time he was twelve he was as big as any man on the plantation, so Old Master sent him to the fields to pick cotton. Most pickers carried one, maybe two bags, but John asked for three—one for each shoulder and one for the middle of his back.

He started at one end of the field and didn't look up until he got to the other end. He bent his back and kept it bent—going up and down those fields as quick as a water bug skimpering across a pond. By the end of the day he'd picked over four thousand pounds of that white fluff—more than three bales. No one had ever been known to pick more than one bale in a day, and when everyone saw what John Henry had done, their eyes got as big as saucers and they asked, "How'd you do that, John?"

"Well," said John, "I can't help it. I'm just a natural man."

John worked on that plantation until the Civil War came and finally put an end to slavery. And then he began to ramble. He rambled far and wide, taking on whatever job had to be done. He worked as a tobacco stripper and as a corn picker for a while, and then he went to work as a deckhand on the steamboats that ran up and down the Mississippi River.

Once, on a wild and stormy night, the beam that drove the paddle wheel broke. The boat was tossed and turned—first this way, then that way—by the waves and wind. It looked like the steamboat and everyone on it was going to pay a visit to the bottom of the Mississippi River.

That is, until John Henry stepped forward. He grabbed the wheel-crank and began to turn it—slow at first, but faster and faster once he found his rhythm. The steamboat began to move again—not under steam power but under John Henry power. All night long he turned that paddle wheel until by morning he brought the steamboat out of the storm and safely into port.

When they asked him, "How'd you do that, John?" he just smiled that big smile of his and said, "I can't help it. I'm just a natural man."

John did well at whatever work he put his hands and his mind to. Sometimes people thought he was a braggart when he'd say what he could do, but that was only until they saw him do it. You see, his *do-so* was always as big as his *say-so*.

But no matter how well John did (and he always did it better than anyone else), he just kept on moving. He was looking for something, but he wasn't sure what it was.

Then one day he heard a ringing coming from over the hill. At first he didn't know what the sound was, but to John Henry it was the sweetest music he'd ever heard. When he reached the top of the hill, he looked down into the valley and he saw what was making that sweet, sweet sound.

It was the ring of steel hitting steel. Dozens of men were swinging hammers, driving steel spikes into the ground to hold down the cross-ties for a railroad. Those men were laying track, and suddenly John Henry knew what he wanted to do. He wanted to be a steel-driving man.

He walked up to the foreman and said, "I'm a natural born steel-drivin' man, and I'm lookin' for a job."

"How much steel-driving you done?" asked the foreman.

"None," answered John Henry, "but that don't matter 'cause I was born knowin' how."

"That ain't good enough around here," said the foreman. "It's hard, dangerous work. Besides, we don't need any braggers on this job."

"Just give me a chance," said John. "I ain't braggin', but the truth is I can drive as much steel as any three men."

Now the way it was done was this: One man, called a shaker, held the spike to the ground. Three men would stand in a circle and take turns hitting that spike with their hammers. When it was all the way in, they'd move on to the

next one. Sometimes the shaker would be holding a six-foot steel drill between his knees. He'd turn it a quarter turn after each blow. The men with the hammers would drive that drill as deep into the ground as they could. Then they'd put dynamite in the hole to blast out the rock for a roadbed or a tunnel.

Being a shaker was a dangerous job. Most hammers weighed nine or ten pounds each, and they came down with tremendous force. If a driver ever missed, there was a good chance that it would mean the end of the shaker.

The foreman decided to give John Henry a chance. He was sure John Henry would make a fool of himself, and everyone else would have a good laugh.

At first none of the shakers wanted to hold the spike, but finally a small man about John Henry's age stepped forward. His name was Little Willie, and he said he'd hold the spike for the stranger.

John Henry picked up a hammer that had been lying on the ground, but it seemed a little light to him. He tried a few others until he found a twelve-pound sheep-nose hammer with a four-foot handle. The handle was thin and limber and greased with tallow to keep it smooth. When it was held straight out the hammer would hang halfway down to the ground.

"Hit it gentle at first," said Little Willie, but John had already begun his swing.

The hammer head touched the back of his knees and then it flashed down so fast no one was sure they had seen it. They heard it ring, though, because it sounded like a church bell on a Sunday morning. Two more swings as quick as lightning, and the spike was all the way in the ground.

The railroad men just stood there with their mouths hanging open, watching the spike smoking from the force of the blows. It took a minute or two before anyone spoke, and then the foreman said, "I've never seen anything like that in all my born days. John Henry, you're hired."

And that's the way John Henry became a steel-driving man. There was never another one like him before that, and there sure isn't going to be another one like him again. He could hammer every which way—up, down, or sideways. Hard rock or soft. It didn't make any difference to him. He could hammer all day long and never miss a stroke.

Of course, Little Willie worked as his shaker from that day on, but sometimes John pounded steel so fast there had to be another man around to throw water on the hammers and the drills so they wouldn't catch fire. It wasn't long before he was swinging two twenty-pound hammers and loving every minute of it.

Sometimes Willie would sing to keep the rhythm and sometimes John Henry would sing:

> *Ain't no hammer*   (Wham!)
> *Rings like mine, Lord*   (Wham!)
> *Rings like gold, Lord*   (Wham!)
> *Ain't it fine.*   (Wham!)

And that song could be heard all up and down the line. When John Henry was feeling extra good—and that was pretty often—it sounded like the mountain was sinking in. But it was only his hammers sucking wind.

Somewhere along the way John Henry met a young woman named Polly Ann. She had gleaming black hair as wavy as the ocean, eyes that sparkled like polished glass, and a dimple in her cheek that came and went like a ruffle on a lake.

He loved her more than his tongue could tell and she loved him the same way, so they did what most folks who love each other do. They got married. And then they did what most married folks do. They had a little baby—a little baby that John Henry could hold in the palm of his hand.

John Henry and Polly Ann and their little baby began to roam. They never stayed in any one place too long, for, you see, John Henry would say what he could do and then he would do it. After all, John Henry was a natural man who said what he meant and meant what he said.

John Henry drove steel in Alabama, Mississippi, Virginia, and Georgia. And if he got sick—which happened sometimes even to him—Polly Ann would take his place and drive steel like a man.

One time, down in Georgia somewhere, John Henry was working on a crew laying track. They still had a hundred feet to go when the foreman saw the 5:15 express coming at them at sixty miles an hour. The sun was shining in the engineer's eyes, and he didn't see the signals telling him to stop. If something wasn't done in a few minutes, there was going to be an awful train wreck.

John Henry saw that train barreling out of the east and he knew just what to do. He told everyone to get out of the way and he went to work—John Henry style. He grabbed two lengths of track a hundred feet long and rolled them into a coil. He swung them around and around and let them fly. They hit the ground flat and lay there as straight as a ruler. Then he picked up two handfuls of railroad spikes and shoved them in his mouth. With a hammer in each hand he began to run down the ties as fast as he could, spitting the spikes through his teeth and smashing them into place with his hammers. The 5:15 got closer and closer, but John Henry drove in those last two spikes and jumped from the track just as the express *(Whoo-Whoo!)* went streaking by. The engineer never even knew he was in danger.

The crew came running up to John, cheering and patting him on the back.

"John Henry," said the foreman, "that's the most amazing thing I've ever seen or dreamed."

"It wasn't so much," said John. "I'm just a natural man, and I can't help it."

The year was 1872. John Henry was thirty-four years old. He and his family were wandering around again, this time in West Virginia, looking for a new job to tackle. Polly Ann loved her man and was mighty proud of him, but she was just like most other mothers. She wanted to settle down, and she told him so.

"John, honey, I wish we could stop our roamin' for a while. I wish we had a house of our own, a place we could raise our child and maybe even a garden."

"Don't you worry none, honey," said John, flashing that special smile of his that made everyone like him so. "This is gonna be a good year for us. I know it because it's 1872."

"What's that got to do with anything?" asked Polly Ann.

"Well," said John, "just look at it. 1872. One and eight are nine, and seven and two are nine, and nine is my lucky number. I weighed thirty-three pounds when I was born. Everyone knows that, and everyone knows that three times three are nine. And besides, there are nine letters in my natural-born name: J-O-H-N-H-E-N-R-Y. Nine. So this is gonna be our lucky year."

And for a while it seemed as if John Henry was right.

For it was there in West Virginia, nine miles east of Hinton and one mile west of Talcott in Summers County, that the Chesapeake & Ohio Railroad had begun to build the longest tunnel that had ever been built. It was to be the Big Bend Tunnel, and it was going to be a mile and a quarter long through solid rock. They decided to call it the Big Bend Tunnel because right there is where the Greenbrier River makes a sharp bend to the south.

When John Henry heard about it, a little shiver went up and down his spine. (Maybe he was remembering what he'd said to his mother when he was still a little baby: "Big Bend Tunnel on the C. and O. 'Road gonna be the death of me.") But he didn't pay it any more mind than a fly touching down on his arm.

He didn't have any trouble getting hired on. Remember, John Henry was simply the finest steel-driving man in the whole, wide world. When Captain Tommy Walters, the foreman, saw what he could do, he gave him four dollars a day, a company house to live in, and all the food that John and Polly Ann and their little baby could eat—and believe you me, that was a mighty heap of food.

Soon Little Willie joined John at the Big Bend Tunnel, and watching them work together you would have thought they were playing. Little Willie would hold the steel and John would drive it. He'd whirl that hammer around his shoulders so fast you'd swear you could hear the thunder behind it. And one or the other of them would always be singing:

> *Oh, this hammer*   (Wham!)
> *Hammer ring*   (Wham!)
> *While I sing, Lord*   (Wham!)
> *Hear me sing!*   (Wham!)

Of course, the work was hard and dangerous. The deeper into the mountain they went, the darker and hotter it got. The air was filled with smoke and dust. Men worked without shirts, and the sweat poured off their backs like streams running downhill. There were lots of cave-ins and lots of accidents, but slowly the work got done and the tunnel got longer and longer.

One day a stranger in a checkered suit and a silk necktie appeared at the tunnel. He was from somewhere up north, and he was there trying to sell a newfangled machine—a steam drill that could drill into rock. Back in those days there weren't too many machines around. There was the cotton gin and a few others, but most work was still done by real live men.

"I've got this steam drill here," said the stranger, "that can outdrill any crew you have. It doesn't get tired. It doesn't have to rest and it doesn't have to eat. It's sure to save you a lot of money."

Captain Tommy looked at the machine. It had a twenty-foot-long boiler, all kinds of levers and gears, and, of course, a big metal rotary drill on one end. All that metal just sat there and gleamed in the sun.

"Mighty pretty," said Captain Tommy. "And it might be a fine machine, but I've got a man here named John Henry who's the finest steel-driving man in the world. He can outdrill any machine that's ever been built."

"I've heard of John Henry," said the man with the steam drill. "I know he's the best, but there's still no man alive who can do more work faster than my drill."

Captain Tommy said he didn't need the drill, but the salesman suggested a race between his machine and John Henry. They would each drill for a full day—and back then a full day was nine hours. If the machine won, Captain Tommy would buy it. If John Henry won, Captain Tommy would get the drill and five hundred dollars.

That seemed like a good idea to Captain Tommy, but he was a fair man and John Henry was his friend. He said he'd have to speak to John first. The Captain told John Henry about the machine and the race, saying he'd give him half the money if he won.

"That's a whole mess of money," said John Henry, "but the money don't matter. What matters is that I'm a natural man who can drive more steel than any nine men who were ever born. A man ain't nothin' but a man, but I got a heart in here," he said, tapping his chest with his huge hands. "A machine ain't nothin' but a machine, and all it's got inside is a metal engine. Cap'n, before I let that steam drill beat me down I'll die with my hammer in my hand."

The day of the race was set. People came from all around —some from as far away as Virginia and Pennsylvania. There were more than two thousand people there that day to see if John Henry meant what he said this time.

Early in the morning John Henry was there on the right side, greasing up the handles of his two twenty-pound hammers. He'd need them both if he was going to beat that machine. Little Willie was there too, getting together all the drills they'd need for the race.

John said to him, "Shaker, you'd better pray, 'cause if I miss this little piece of steel, tomorrow'll be your buryin' day."

"I ain't worried," said Little Willie. "You ain't missed yet, and I don't believe you're gonna miss today."

On the left was the steam drill. Men were running around it, squirting it here and there with oil and grease. Beside the machine was a big pile of pine knots to fire it with.

For a minute everything was as quiet as rock dust settling in a drill hole. Then Captain Tommy fired his pistol, and the race was on.

Men shoveled pine into the steam drill's boiler. It groaned and it moaned and then it started to move. *Chugga-Chugga-Chugga-Chugga-Chugga.* The big mechanical drill began pumping up and down, eating away at the rock like a hungry man going at a plate of ribs.

John Henry started swinging his hammers, finding his own rhythm. *Wham! Wham! Wham!* They rang like silver against the drill.

"How we doin'?" asked John after the first hour.

"The steam drill's ahead," answered Little Willie.

"Don't worry none," said John, "I'm just warmin' up."

Steel met steel, and by the end of the second hour sparks were flying fast and hot. John Henry's hammers began to heat up and glow, and men had to throw water over them to keep them from catching fire. But the steam drill kept pounding into rock and it stayed ahead.

Then in the third hour the machine stopped chugging. One of the gears broke and had to be repaired. John Henry didn't stop though. His hammers kept whirring through the air like giant hummingbirds. For a while the only sounds in those hills were Little Willie's song and the *Wham! Wham! Wham!* of John's hammers. Willie kept singing and John kept swinging, and before the machine was fixed John pulled ahead.

A great cheer came from the crowd. "Keep it up, John. Keep it up!" they shouted. Just about everyone—everyone, that is, but the stranger who'd brought the steam drill— wanted John to win. He was a man and they loved him, and who ever heard of anyone loving a machine?

And keep it up he did—even when the machine started again with a roar and a hiss. Steam whistled out of the boiler, and the giant drill bit into the hard rock. *Chugga-Chugga-Chugga-Chugga.*

Four hours, five hours, six hours. The sun rose higher into the bright sky until it passed overhead and began reaching toward the west. John Henry stayed ahead of the steam drill. Little Willie was gray with the dust that came flying out of the holes, but he kept turning that drill.

"How you feelin'?" he screamed over the whining and chugging of the machine.

"I still feel like the sunrise," shouted John. "Just keep singin'."

> *Take this hammer*   (Wham!)
> *Carry it to the Captain.*   (Wham!)

Seven hours, eight hours. The sun was sinking fast. Sweat poured off John Henry's muscles and steam rose from his body, but he just kept on driving.

"How you feelin' now?" asked Little Willie as they began the ninth and final hour.

John Henry didn't answer this time. He was one with his hammers, swinging them again and again, making them ring like gold. Then the sun slipped behind the mountain, and Captain Tommy's pistol rang out. The race was over.

The steam drill chugged a few last chugs, and suddenly everything was as still as the bottom of a pond on a moonless night. The judges rushed forward to measure the holes. Everyone's eyes were on them.

"John Henry's holes measure seven feet each," they announced. "John Henry made fourteen feet. The steam drill only made nine."

A great cheer rose up and shook the mountain. John Henry had done what he had said he would. He had beaten the steam drill.

But when they all turned to look at him, John Henry was lying on the ground, staring up at the sky. His hammers were still in his hands. Pretty Polly Ann was kneeling beside him crying small, silent tears. He turned his head to her and said, "I had to do it, honey. I'm just a natural-born steel-drivin' man, and I couldn't help it."

Then John Henry laid down his hammers and he died. He had beat that machine, but he broke his poor heart doing it.

They buried him right there in the sand by the Big Bend Tunnel. On his tombstone they wrote, "HERE LIES A STEEL-DRIVING MAN."

John Henry was the last man to beat a machine, and a lot of folks say if he were alive today he would still do it—or die trying.

Those folks also say that if you go to the Big Bend Tunnel at the break of day, you can still hear John Henry's hammers ring.

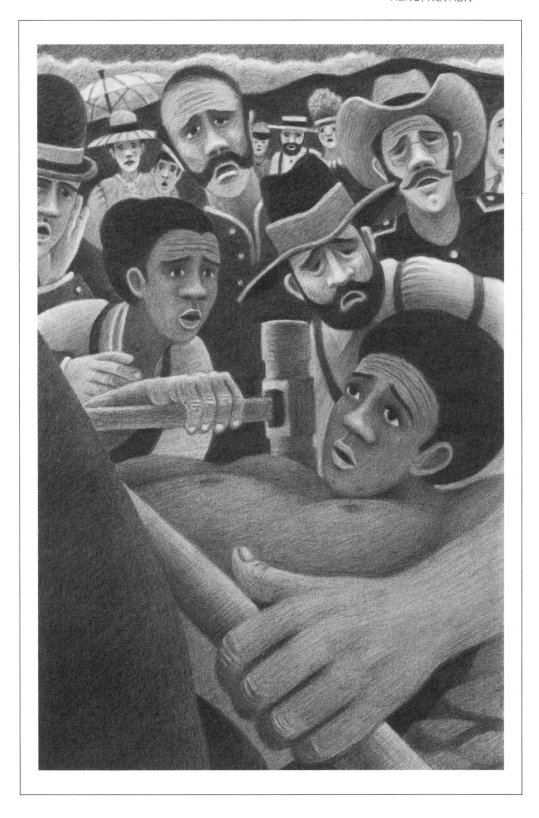

John Henry

Traditional

When John Hen-ry was a lit-tle ba-by,—

Set-tin' on his mam-my's knee,— Said,

"Big Bend — Tun-nel on the C. and O. — 'Road,

Gon-na be the death – of — me, Lord, – Lord,

Gon-na be the death – of — me." Said, me."

When John Henry was a little baby,
Settin' on his mammy's knee,
Said, "Big Bend Tunnel on the C. and O. 'Road,
Gonna be the death of me, Lord, Lord,
Gonna be the death of me."

Now John Henry had a little woman,
Her name was Polly Ann,
When John Henry took sick and had to go to bed,
Polly Ann drove steel like a man, Lord, Lord,
Polly Ann drove steel like a man!

The captain said to John Henry,
"I'm gonna bring that steel drill 'round,
I'm gonna bring that steel drill out on the job,
Gonna whop that steel on down, Lord, Lord,
Gonna whop that steel on down."

Well, John Henry said to his captain,
"Lord, a man ain't nothin' but a man,
But before I let your steam drill beat me down,
I'll die with a hammer in my hand, Lord, Lord,
I'll die with a hammer in my hand."

John Henry said to his shaker,
"Shaker, you'd better pray,
If my hammer misses that little piece of steel,
Tomorrow'll be your buryin' day, Lord, Lord,
Tomorrow'll be your buryin' day."

Now the captain said to John Henry,
"I believe this mountain's sinkin' in."
John Henry just laughed at his captain and he said,
"Ain't nothin' but my hammer suckin' wind, Lord, Lord,
Ain't nothin' but my hammer suckin' wind."

John Henry said to his shaker,
"Shaker, why don't you sing?
I'm throwin' twenty pounds from my hips on down,
Just listen to that cold steel ring, Lord, Lord,
Just listen to that cold steel ring."

Now the man that invented the steam drill,
He thought he was mighty fine,
But John Henry drove fourteen feet,
And the steam drill only made nine, Lord, Lord,
And the steam drill only made nine.

John Henry hammered on the mountain,
And his hammer was striking fire,
But he drove so hard that he broke his poor heart,
And he laid down his hammer and he died, Lord, Lord,
He laid down his hammer and he died.

John Henry had a little baby,
He could hold him in the palm of his hand,
And the last words I heard that poor boy say,
"My daddy was a steel-drivin' man, Lord, Lord,
My daddy was a steel-drivin' man."

Well, they took John Henry to the tunnel,
And they buried him in the sand,
Every locomotive comes rollin' by
Says, "There lies a steel-drivin' man, Lord, Lord,
There lies a steel-drivin' man."

So every Monday morning,
When the bluebirds begin to sing,
You can hear those hammers a mile or more,
You can hear John Henry's hammer ring, Lord, Lord,
You can hear John Henry's hammer ring.

NOTE: There are over fifty versions of the John Henry ballad. This one has been compiled by the author.